Contents

Letts

AGES 8–9
KEY STAGE 2

Premier I.C.T.

Toolbars

Here are the toolbars you usually see when you open a program.

Standard toolbar

Formatting toolbar

To add extra menu buttons, point with the mouse pointer here and click the left mouse button once. Choose **Add or Remove Buttons**.

For some activities, you will also need the drawing tools.

To add the Drawing toolbar to the screen, open the **View** menu, choose **Toolbars** and tick **Drawing**.

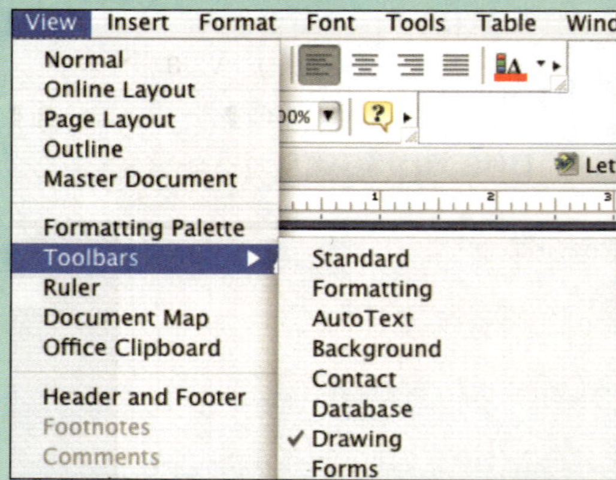

I Practise viewing the different toolbars.

a Use the **View** menu to add the following toolbars to the screen:

Drawing *Picture* *WordArt*

b Now remove the **Picture** and **WordArt** toolbars, but leave the **Drawing** toolbar on screen.

c Set the **Standard** toolbar to show these buttons:

II Which toolbar do these buttons belong to – Standard, Formatting or Drawing?

a 

____

c 

____

e 

____

b 

____

d 

____

f 

____

Saving and Printing

Make a folder to save your work:

- Click the left mouse button once on **Start**, go to **Documents** and click the left mouse button again.
- Select **My Documents**, open the **File** menu and select **New** then **Folder** by clicking the left mouse button once. 

- Type your name in the highlighted **New Folder** box and press the **enter** key on the keyboard or click anywhere on the screen with the left mouse button.

To **Save** something for the first time, when you have started a new piece of work:

- Open **Word** and type a sentence.
- Open the **File** menu and choose **Save As**.
- Place the screen arrow on **My Documents** and left mouse click once to open it.
- Click the left mouse button twice on your folder to open it.
- Give your work a **File Name** and click **Save** using the left mouse button.

It is important to save work regularly. Each time you add something or change your work, point to the  button on the toolbar and click the left mouse button once. Don't wait until you have finished!

To **Print**, open the **File** menu and choose **Print** to see the **Print** menu box. Make sure you have selected the correct printer and number of copies and click **OK** with your left mouse button.

I Make a folder for your work.

a Write six sentences about your favourite TV programme.

b **Save** it in your folder.

c Give your work the file name: 'TV News'.

d **Save** all the work you do in this book in your folder.

II Answer these questions about saving and printing.

a What would you store in a folder? Circle the correct answer.

Names *Lists* *Files*

b Why do you think it is important to save your work each time you add or change something?

____

c How does it help to put all your work in the same folder?

____

Important text

To show that text is important, change the **Font** and **Size** or make it **Bold**.

To make changes to the text, you need to highlight the typed text by holding the left mouse button and dragging the mouse pointer across it first.

- To change the **Font**, point here [Times ▾] using the mouse and left click once. Roll the mouse pointer down the list. Use the scroll bar to see more fonts. Left click on a font to choose it.
- Select a size in the same way that you selected a new font here: [12 ▾].
- To make the text **Bold**, point and click with the mouse here: [**B**].

Party Invitation
Please come to my party on
Saturday 27th September
2.30 – 4.30pm
at the
Dining Dinosaurs Fun Den
r.s.v.p. Alisha

I **Type these class rules for using a computer. Make the most important rules bigger and bolder.**

Put up your hand if you need help.
Stop and ask if you don't understand.
Shut down the computer at the end of a lesson.
Follow the worksheet and computer instructions carefully.
Do not touch the monitor screen.
If something goes wrong, leave it alone and tell the teacher.
Ask the teacher before you print.
Do not hang on to the mouse when it is someone else's turn.

II **Look through the drop down menus on the toolbar.**

File	Edit	View	Insert	Format	Tools	Table	Window	Help

a Which menu would you use to change the text to a different style?

____

b What else can you change using the **Font** menu box?

____

c Which words look important on the party invitation above?

__________ __________ __________

Cut and Paste

Cut and **Paste** are useful tools when you want to move words or chunks of text from one place to another.

The events in this story have been typed in the wrong order:

> Next I went around the back of the house to the kitchen, but that was empty too. First I tried the door, but it was locked. Finally I tried a neighbour's house to see if anyone could help me. Then I looked through the letterbox, but I couldn't see anyone in the hall.

To move the text:

- Highlight this sentence:
  First I tried the door, but it was locked.
- Open the **Edit** menu and select **Cut**.
- Point the mouse pointer where you want to place the sentence and click the left mouse button once: |Next.
- Open the **Edit** menu and select **Paste**.
- Now move this sentence using **Cut** and **Paste**:
  Then I looked through the letterbox, but I couldn't see anyone in the hall.
- Place it after these words: *empty too.*

I **These school memories are in the wrong order. Type all of them, then use Cut and Paste to put them in the right order.**

a We visited Sherwood Forest on my sixth birthday in Class 2.

b I started school when I was five, well almost five.

c Next I moved to Class 2.

d When I was seven, I moved up to Class 3 with my best friend, Saika.

e My first class teacher was Mrs Scott.

What is the correct order? _____ _____ _____ _____ _____

II **Instead of using the Edit menu to Cut and Paste, you can use the buttons on the toolbar, or you can use a keyboard shortcut by pressing and holding the Ctrl key with a letter key. Use the Edit menu to help you answer these questions:**

a Circle the button you would use for **Cut**.

b Circle the button you would use for **Paste**.

c Which keyboard shortcut would you use for **Cut**? **Ctrl** + _____

d Which keyboard shortcut would you use for **Paste**? **Ctrl** + _____

Improving text

A computer's thesaurus helps you to change words quickly by finding more interesting ones with the same meaning to use in your writing. These are called *synonyms*.

- Type the sentence: It was a **nice** day.
- Highlight a word, e.g. **nice**.
- Open the **Tools** menu.
- Select **Language**, then **Thesaurus** and left mouse click to open it.
- Look carefully through the new words.
- Click on a word you think would be better, e.g. *pleasant*, but only choose a word you understand.
- Left mouse click on **Replace**.
- The sentence changes to: It was a **pleasant** day.

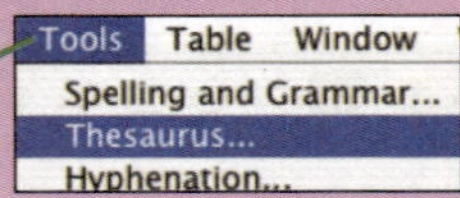

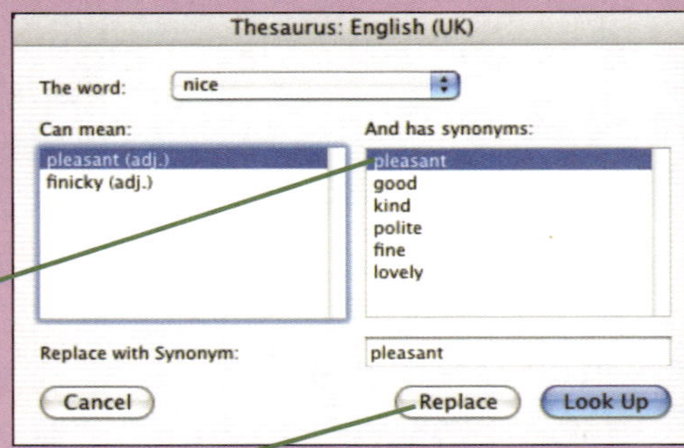

Sometimes the thesaurus gives you *antonyms*. These are words with the opposite meaning.

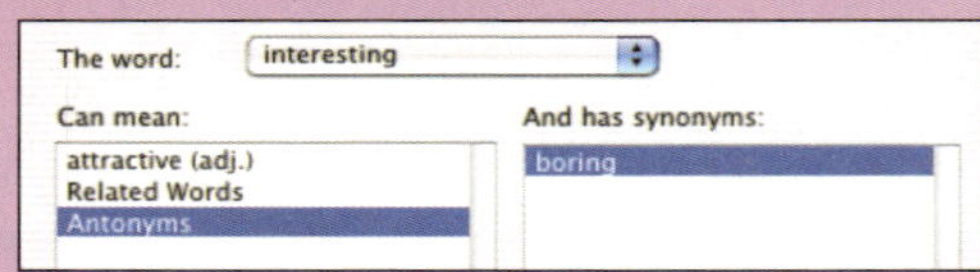

I **Type the words in red and look them up in the computer's Thesaurus. Circle any of the *synonyms* you found.**

a cold	*chilly*	*frosty*	*sizzling*
b nice	*terrible*	*lovely*	*fine*
c good	*enjoyable*	*disagreeable*	*excellent*
d happy	*cheerful*	*sad*	*contented*
e sad	*contented*	*gloomy*	*miserable*

II **Change the mood of this story by using the Thesaurus to find words that mean the *opposite* of the words in italic. Cross out the italic words and write the *antonyms* in the *blank* spaces.**

The day had been *terrible* ______________. The party was *boring* ______________. Everyone had gone home *dejected* ______________. Now it was over, Sally was *delighted* ______________.

Making corrections

Correct mistakes quickly and easily using a spell checker or the keyboard.

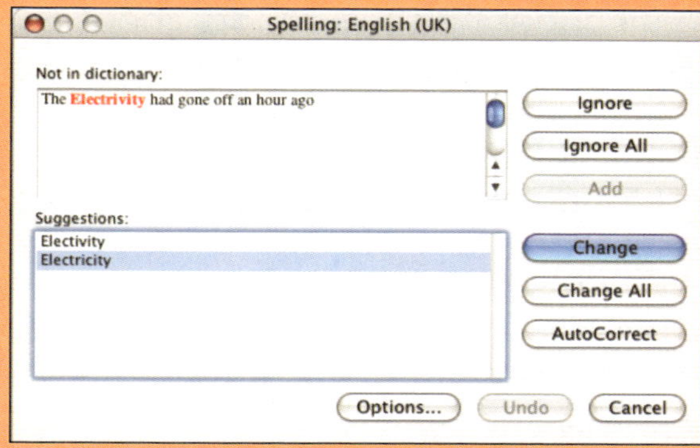

When you have finished typing:

- Open the **Tools** menu and choose **Spelling** or left mouse click on this button on the toolbar: .
- A 'mistake' is shown in the top box. Does it need changing?
- If the answer is yes, roll the mouse pointer over the suggestions underneath, left mouse click on the correct spelling and choose **Change**.

Take care: the first suggestion is not always the right one. Remember that the spell checker only recognises spelling mistakes.

It might not find the mistake in this sentence: '*He **hopped** his birthday would come soon*', because 'hopped' is a proper word, not a spelling mistake.

Other ways to make corrections to text include:

- Using the **backspace key** to delete a letter or a word.
- Using **Undo** 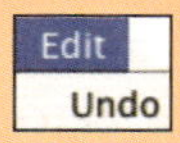

 or  to undo the last thing you did.
- Using typeover – highlight a word and type the new word over it.

I **Type the text exactly as it is shown in the box. Use a spell checker to help you to find five mistakes.**

Underline the mistakes in the text. Which mistake did the **spell checker** miss?

Danny's class were having a competition to desine a moneybox, so Danny asked if he could look in his Dad's shed for some idaes. His freind Peter came around to help. At the bottom of an old cuboard, Danny found just what he was looking four.

The **spell checker** missed: ______________

II **Most word processors put a red or green wavy line under a mistake as you type.**

a What do you think the red line means?

____

b What do you think the green line means?

____

Find and Replace

A local paper had this report about Sam. It was a good report – except that Sam was a girl!

Instead of typing the whole story again, the reporter used **Find** and **Replace** to make the changes.

To use **Find** and **Replace**:

- Open the **Edit** menu, choose **Replace.**
- In the **Find what** box, type the word you want to change.
- In the **Replace with** box, type the replacement word.
- Choose **Replace.**
- Now left click on **Find Next** until there are no more words left to change.

Don't be tempted to use **Replace All** – you may find that the word **here** becomes **shere**!

> Local artist, Sam, has loved drawing since he was little and now he has won first prize in our poster competition. His mum said she was really proud of him. All of us here are too. Congratulations, Sam!

I Type these sentences.

I was going on a school trip for five days. I had to pack my case, sort out my spending money, have my hair cut and tidy my room, but how would I have time for all that?

a Change some of the words in this story to make it a story about a girl called Lee. Use **Find** and **Replace**. Write down the words that you changed. **Save As**: Lee.

____

b Open the story about Lee and use **Find** and **Replace** to change it to a story about a boy called Lee. Write down the words that you changed this time.

____

II Look at the text below. Fill in the blank spaces with the words in the box.

Replace	missing	Find	Edit

To ____________ and ____________ a word, open the ____________ menu and choose ____________. Type the word you want to change in the '____________ what' box. Type the new word in the '____________ with' box. Click ____________. ____________ and ____________ finds and changes words easily, without ____________ any!

Alignment

Alignment describes how text or graphics are positioned on a page.

Text placed to the left has a straight left edge and a jagged right edge.

BRING AND BUY

St. Andrew's Hall
9.30 – 11.30 am
Saturday 10th April

Please come and support us

Organisers:
Kalinda and Claire

In aid of
The Children's Hospital
Tel: 352917

Text that is centred is placed in the middle of the line with an equal space either side.

Text placed to the right has a straight right edge and a jagged left edge.

To align text:

- Type the text and highlight it.
- Open the **Format** menu and choose **Paragraph, Indents and Spacing**, then **Alignment, left, right** or **centre**; or use the shortcuts on the **Formatting toolbar:** left , right or centre .

I Type a thank-you letter.

Position your text *left* (4,5), *right* (1,2) or *centre* (3).

26 Main Road
Tollbridge — 1

12th November 2003 — 2

4 — Dear Auntie Carol

5 — Thank you so much for my birthday present. It was just what I wanted. I wore it at my party and have worn it every day since. Here's a photo for you.

Love from
Billy — 3

II How would you align the text for:

a Stories? ______________ b Headings? ______________

c The sender's address on a party invitation? ______________

Bullets and Numbering

Bullets and **Numbering** are used for lists: on posters, in books or for a list of instructions.

To create a bulleted list:

- Type *
- Press the **space bar** or the **tab** key.
- Type your text.
- Press the **enter** key. Look how the computer automatically creates a list.
- Press the **enter** key after typing each item on the list.
- Press the **enter** key twice to finish the list.

Summer Fair

13th July

- Book Stall
- Cake Stall
- Raffle
- Games

Learning Spellings

1 Look at a word.
2 Cover it.
3 Write it.
4 Check it.

A numbered list is created in the same way by typing 1 instead of * (but you must press the **tab** key afterwards, not the **space bar**).

To add bullets or numbers to a list that is already typed, highlight the list, and left mouse click on the buttons on the **Formatting toolbar** for **Numbering** or for **Bullets**.

I Practise making bulleted and numbered lists.

a Type this text as a **bulleted** list.

In my packed lunch box I have sandwiches, a packet of crisps, an apple, a chocolate bar and a carton of juice.

b Type these instructions as a **numbered** list.

To make a cup of tea I need to boil the kettle, warm the teapot, put the teabag in the teapot, add the boiling water to the teapot, let it stand for two minutes, put some milk in a cup, and pour the tea into the cup.

II What can you find out about bullets?

a Using the drop down menu, you can choose different styles of **bullets**. Circle the menu you would use to find **bullets**.

File	Edit	View	Insert	Format	Tools	Table	Window	Help

b If you customise a **bullet**, you can change the colour and size. What else can you do to it?

____

Labels

Text boxes are really useful for creating labels and captions. They can be moved and placed anywhere on the page, and any text inside moves with them.

Creating a text box:

- Type and highlight the text.
- Open the **Insert** menu and choose **Text Box**.
- Drag the handles of the box to resize it so that you can see all the text.

Using a text box:

- Left mouse click inside the box to type.
- Change the font, size and colour of text using the tools on the **Formatting** toolbar: Times 12 A.
- Point to the border with the mouse pointer and left mouse click – the pointer changes to four arrows. Drag to move the box.

I Make some labels for a history project.

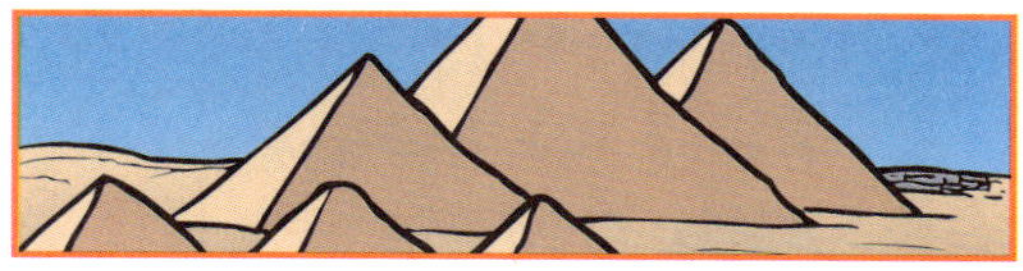

a Type this text: *History Project*
The Ancient Egyptians

b Highlight the text, and place it in a text box. Change the font and size of the title. Resize the box and move it to the centre of the page.

c Add another text box underneath with your name in. Now you have a cover sheet for your project. Add some more pages with labels.

II Text box crossword.

Across

1 Do this to the text before you add a text box.
4 The border is made of these when you click inside a text box.
5 Text boxes are useful for creating these.
7 The border is made of these when you click on it.

Down

2 Open this menu to add a text box.
3 Drag this to make the text box bigger – or smaller!
4 Which toolbar has a [button icon] button?
6 Make a label using a text________.

Newspapers

Newspapers use different **Sizes** and **Fonts** for headings, sub-headings and story text. In a newspaper, the main story always has a bigger heading than the others; the words you use should 'grab your attention' as well!

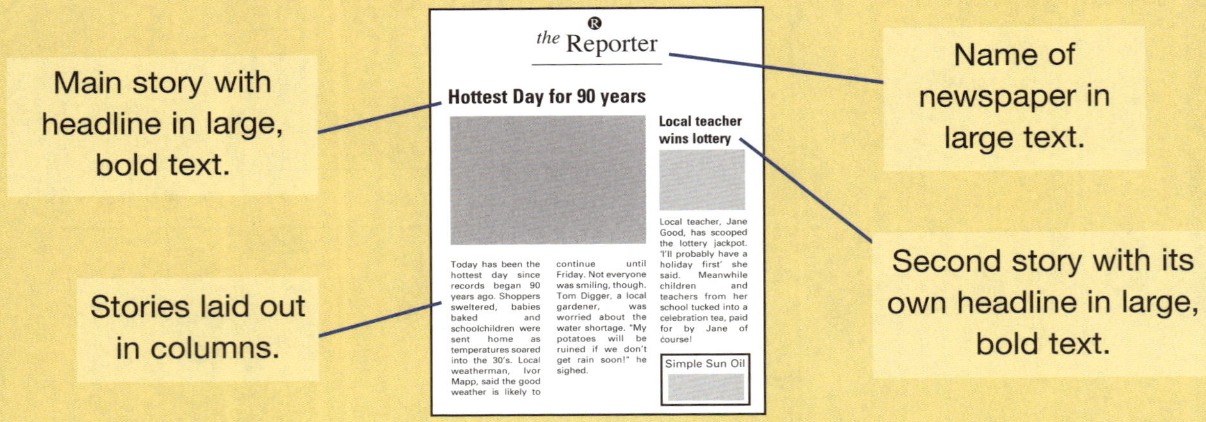

A newspaper is a good example of how text and graphics can be used together. To write your own newspaper article, work on the news items first, use the **Thesaurus** to make a story even better and **Spell Check** everything – newspaper readers will always spot mistakes!

To organise the text into Columns use the shortcut button on the **toolbar** or:

- Highlight the text.
- Open the **Format** menu and choose **Columns**.
- Choose two or three columns and left mouse click **OK**.

I Type a story for a school newspaper. Here are some tools that you should use.

- Make the heading stand out by increasing the text size and putting it in bold.
- Organise the text into columns.
- Read and improve the words in the story, by using the **Thesaurus**.
- Check the spelling.
- Save the story in your work folder.

II Complete the sentences by circling the correct ending.

a Newspaper stories are laid out in *headlines* *story text* *columns*.

b The newspaper in the introduction has *two* *three* *four* columns.

c Use different sizes and fonts to *check spellings* *make the text look more important* *organise the columns*.

d The most 'eye catching' text should be the *headlines* *stories* *adverts*.

Adding graphics

Improve the look of text with graphics.

Add photos or images from the computer's **Clip Art** gallery or a **Clip Art** CD-ROM. Alternatively, use a scanner to add photos or images from magazines or an ordinary camera. Download photos from a digital camera and import them into a piece of written work.

To add a picture from Clip Art:

- Open the **Insert** menu.
- Choose

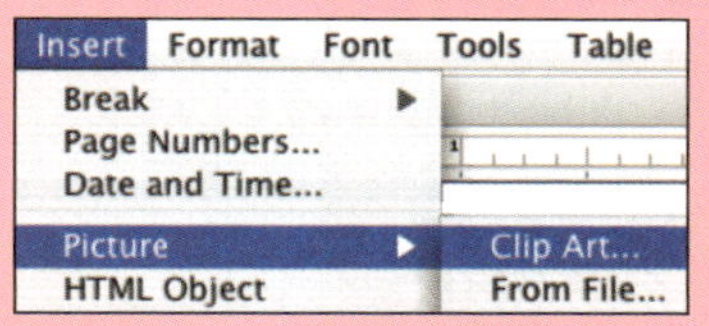

  and left click with the mouse.
- **Search** the Clip Art gallery.
- Double left mouse click on a picture, then click on the insert button that appears to add it to your work.

To add a picture from a Clip Art CD-ROM:

- Put the CD-ROM in the CD drive.
- Open the **Insert** menu.
- Choose **Picture**, from **File** and left click with the mouse.
- Open the menu **Look in** and double left mouse click on the CD drive to open the CD-ROM.
- Search the CD-ROM, highlight a picture and add it by double clicking the left mouse button.

Use the software that has been put onto your computer for a scanner or digital camera to send a picture straight to **Word**.

I Add graphics to a story.

a Open the newspaper story you have written and saved from page 12.

b Add a picture from the computer's **Clip Art** gallery or a **Clip Art** CD-ROM.

c If you have a scanner attached to your computer, open the scanner program using **Start** and the **Programs** menu. Place a photo on the scanner and choose **Scan to Word**. Follow the instructions on-screen for scanning. (You may need to ask for adult help with this.)

II Name three different ways to add a picture to a piece of writing.

a ____________ b ____________ c ____________

d What do you need on your computer to be able to use a scanner or a digital camera?

____

e Explain how to find a picture in **Clip Art**.

____

____

Creative drawings

Create your own graphics and illustrations using the **Drawing** tools.

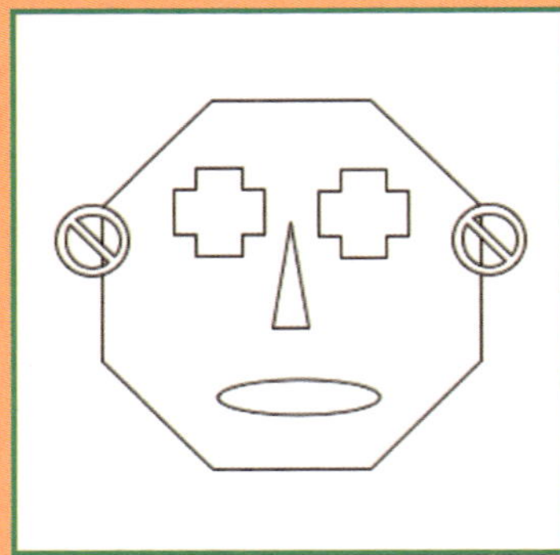

- Open the **Drawing** toolbar in Word (**View, Toolbars** and click on **Drawing**).
- Add shapes to the page from **Autoshapes** and use them to make a picture. To move each shape, put the mouse pointer over it and left click the mouse to highlight it, press and hold the left mouse button and drag the shape into place.
- Highlight each shape and fill with colour  or change the line colour .
- To join the shapes, point and left click the mouse on **Select Objects**  and drag a dotted line around the picture by pressing and holding the left mouse button.
- Open the **Draw** menu and choose 

. Left mouse click  again.

Add your graphics to stories, poems or pieces of non-fiction writing.

I Make an identity card for an extra-terrestrial.

a Use the **Drawing** tools to create a passport photo.

b Use **Word** to create the text.

Name

____

Place of Birth

____

Home Planet

____

II Here are some Drawing tools. What are they used for?

a 

____

b 

____

c 

____

d 

____

e 

____

f 

____

Scanned images

Use a scanner to scan hand-drawn pictures into **Paint**.

- Draw a simple outline on white paper – use a template if it helps.
- Place the drawing face-down on the scanner.
- Open the scanning software using **Start** and the **Programs** menu. Choose to send the image to **Paint** and left mouse click on **Scan**.
- Check the image on screen. Repair any gaps using the **Brush** tool to stop the colour 'leaking' and **Save As** 'image1'.
- Add extra lines around the picture using the **Brush** tool to create your own stained glass window and **Save As** 'image2'.

- Add colour using the **Fill** tool. Remember to open the **Edit** menu and use **Undo** (or use the toolbar shortcut) if you make a mistake.
- **Save As** 'image3' and **Print**.

To be able to use a scanner you need special software that is installed on the computer when the scanner is connected. The software allows the scanner to scan photos or pictures. It sends digital images to the computer. These are saved as graphic files. Save graphic images as **jpegs** as these types of files take up less memory on the computer.

I Make your own stained glass window picture using a scanner and Paint.

a Draw the outline of a person. Keep it simple.

b Scan your outline into **Paint** and add more lines. It should look like a puzzle that has been joined together. Add colour.

c Make a set of windows for different celebrations: Easter, Christmas, Hallowe'en, Hanukkah, Eid.

II Answer these clues to complete the crossword.

1 Use this device to capture images.

2 Use _______ and **Programs** to find and open the scanning software.

3 (Across then down) To _______ an image to the computer using a scanner you can _______ it.

4 **Save** a file as a _______.

5 _______ any gaps to stop the colour 'leaking'.

Brush strokes

Create your own pictures using the **Paint** tools.

This picture was created using the **Brush** tool and dots of different sizes.

It might help to make a hand-drawn sketch of the shape you want to create. Look at the colour box and decide which colours you are going to use. Keep it simple.

- Open **Paint**.
- Select the **Brush** tool.
- Change the size and shape of the brush by choosing one of these options.
- Click the left mouse button to place the dots on the 'canvas'. Create your picture, starting with the outline shape.

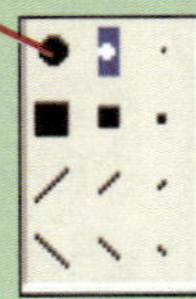

- Change colour by using the colour box.
- Open the **Edit** menu and choose **Undo** to go back a step straight away if you make a mistake. It is much better than using the rubber!
- **Save** the picture in your folder.

I Open a Paint program and use the Brush tool to create a 'dotty' shape.

Use **Copy**, **Paste** and **Resize** to create a group picture. Choose colours that go well together.

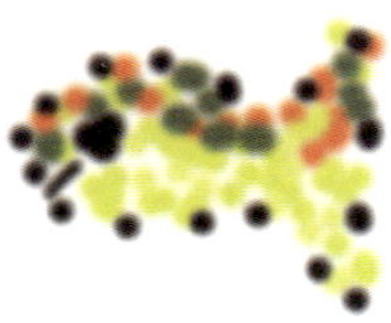

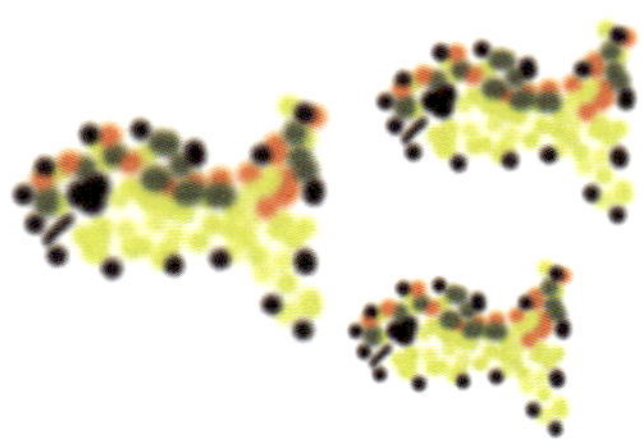

II Draw lines to connect the correct ending to these sentences.

a It is helpful to draw an outline	colour box.
b You can alter the	sketch first.
c To change colour, use the	size and shape of the **Brush** tool.
d To go back a step or correct a mistake	save your work.
e Always remember to	open the **Edit** menu and choose Undo.

Helpful hints

To **Cut** and **Paste**

- Highlight the word or words.
- Use and .
- Or try this shortcut:
  Ctrl key + X to **Cut**
  Ctrl key + V to **Paste**

Helpful hints

- Type a list then highlight it. Click on **Bullets** or **Numbers** to turn it into a numbered or bulleted list.
- Highlight key words or important words and use Bold or change the size to make them stand out.

Helpful hints

To make a folder:

- Left mouse click on **Start**; click **Documents**, then **My Documents**.
- From the **File** menu choose **New**, **Folder**.
- Type your name in the Folder box and left mouse click.

To save work:

- Open the **File** menu; click on **Save As**.
- Find your folder in **My Documents**; double click on it.
- Give the work a file name; click on **Save**.

Helpful hints

- Create a text box using the **Insert** menu.
- Click inside the box to add text and colour .
- Click on the border to add colour and to change the line style.

Helpful hints

- Think about where to place the text in the letter.
- Use the toolbar buttons to align the text left, centre or right.
- Click to print or use the shortcut Ctrl + P.

Helpful hints

To type over a word: Double click on a word and type a new word over it to replace it.

To find and use different words with the same meaning, highlight the word and use the computer's Thesaurus to replace it with another word: from the **Tools** menu, choose **Language**, then **Thesaurus**.

Helpful hints

- To open **Paint**: left mouse click on **Start**, **Programs**, **Accessories** and **Paint**.
- Place the leaves carefully on the scanner and scan to **Paint**.
- Add colour using the **Fill** tool. Experiment with different colours. Click **Edit** and **Undo** to go back a step if you make a mistake.

Helpful hints

- Organise text into columns using the columns tool .
- Make headings stand out with a bigger size text and a different font.
- Use **Zoom** (Whole Page / Two Pages) to see the whole page.
- Check spellings using .

Helpful hints

Add pictures from Clip Art using the **Insert** menu.

To resize a picture:

- Left mouse click once on the picture to highlight it.
- Drag a black corner handle.

or

- Double click on the picture.
- Choose **Layout**, select a wrapping style, click **OK** and drag a corner handle.

Saving work

- Make a folder to save your work.
- Now try it out – type the blurb for a book you have read.
- Save it as a document in your folder.
- Give it the file name: 'Blurb'.

Favourite game

- Do you have a favourite game?
- Write a list of instructions telling a friend how to play it.

Wish list

Type a list of things you would buy if you had £200.

Use **Cut** and **Paste** to put them in order starting with your favourite, then your next favourite and so on.

New words for old

Type this paragraph. Change the words in italic to more interesting words.

Danny had a *nice* birthday. The party food was *really nice*. Everyone had brought him a really *nice* present.

"That was a *good* birthday, the best I've ever had," he said to his mum.

Fan letter

Write a letter to your favourite author about their latest book.

Type your address. Add a couple of paragraphs saying why you like the author's books and why you like this book in particular.

Labels

Make some labels for your school folders, for a project or for a scrapbook:

HOLLY JAMES
HISTORY PROJECT
THE ANCIENT EGYPTIANS

Party invitation

Design an invitation for a party.

Use different sizes of text and add some Clip Art pictures.

Newspaper

- Design the front page of a newspaper.
- Write a main story about a recent event.
- Write a second story about school uniforms, games or school dinners.
- Add pictures from a digital camera or Clip Art.

Leaf patterns

Create a leaf pattern using scanned leaves and **Paint**.

Add extra colours for special effects.

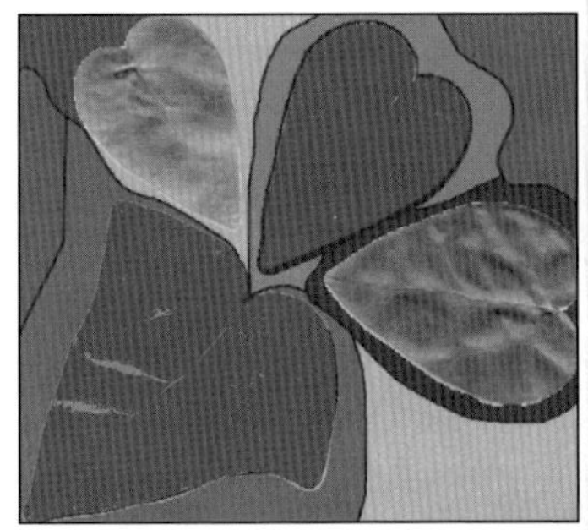

Flowers

Use the **Brush** tool and **Spray Can** to design a delicate flower arrangement for a birthday card.

Place mat

Make a repeat pattern using a simple tile or Clip Art image. Add a border.

Print it, stick it onto card and laminate it to make a place mat or a mouse mat.

Holiday favourites

This table shows where 28 children spent their holidays. Use the information to draw a pie chart.

Place	Number
Spain	12
Canaries	5
Greece	3
UK	5
USA	2
Other	1

Pocket money challenge

Create a pocket money pie chart and answer these questions:

	£
savings	1.00
sweets	1.50
phone card	5.00
cinema	2.50

a What percentage of the money is spent on the phone card?

b What percentage of the money is spent on sweets?

Height chart

This table shows a girl's height from the age of 5 to 8.

Use the information to draw a line chart.

5	6	7	8
105 cm	118 cm	123 cm	128 cm

Let's find out

Use a CD-ROM or the www to find out:

a When the first ancient Olympic Games were held.

b What a baby kangaroo is called.

c Who was the first man to walk on the moon?

Cyber quest

E-mail a local museum or an online museum asking for information about a particular topic – perhaps one you are studying in school.

Use any information they send you, for your project work.

My family

Find out some information about your family for a database.

Name	Age	Favourite colour	Favourite food	Doesn't like…
Mum				
Dad				

Turtle shapes

Type a set of instructions for a screen turtle to draw:

a A triangle with equal sides of 150.

b A pentagon (5 sides) with equal sides of 60.

Helpful hints

- Type the information into **Excel**.
- Highlight the information.
- Use the **Chart Wizard** to help you create a pie chart.

Helpful hints

Look at Rangoli patterns or William Morris patterns for ideas (check these out on the Internet).

Use **Copy** and **Paste** to create a repeat pattern with Clip Art images – use shapes, or objects such as fruit, or a design of your own!

Helpful hints

Use a small brush tool to draw the stems. Select the **Spray Can** tool and tap the mouse button lightly to create a light, flowery effect at the end of each stem.

Helpful hints

Type key words into the **Search** box. Make searches more accurate using 'and' or '+': e.g. Ancient Olympic games + history.

Answers:
a 776 BC
b A joey
c Neil Armstrong

Helpful hints

- Type the information into **Excel**, highlight it and use the **Chart Wizard** to create a line graph.
- Use the **Formatting** tools to change the font, size and colour of the text and the **Drawing** tools to change the background or line colour of the graph.

Helpful hints

- Type the information into **Excel**, highlight it and use the **Chart Wizard** to create a pie chart.
- Use the **Data Labels** to add percentages to the chart.

Answers:
a 50%
b 15%

Helpful hints

To work out the number of degrees in each turn for a regular shape, divide 360 by the number of sides in the shape.

Use **Repeat** to draw regular shapes.

a REPEAT 3 (↑150 forward, →120 right)

b REPEAT 5 (↑60 forward, →72 right)

Helpful hints

Design a questionnaire to help you to collect your answers.

Add the **Table** toolbar to the screen using **View**, **Toolbars** and tick **Tables**.

- **Insert** a table and choose 5 coloumns and 6 rows.
- Add information from your questionnaire.
- Highlight a column and sort using .

Helpful hints

- Do not give out any personal information, e.g. your address.
- Ask an adult to help you to find a trustworthy and reliable museum to contact.
- Search for online museums using the Search box or look through the 24-hour museum website www.24hourmuseum.org.uk

Repeat patterns

Use the **Copy** and **Paste** tools to create a repeat pattern:

- Open **Word** and add a shape to your page (see page 14 to remember how to do this).

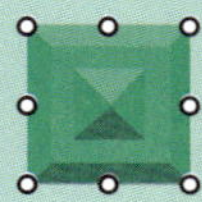

- **Format** it to see the handles.
- **Resize** it if it is too big.
- Highlight the shape, open the **Edit** menu and choose **Copy** or left mouse click on this button.
- Open the **Edit** menu and choose **Paste** or left mouse click on this button.

Repeat until you have six shapes on the page. Highlight each shape and use the mouse to drag it into a position to make a pattern.

Look at page 14 to remember how to **group shapes**.

To **Highlight** a picture:
Place the cursor over the picture and click the left mouse button once.

To **Format** a picture:
Double left click with the mouse on the picture, choose **Layout**, and a wrapping style such as tight. Left mouse click **OK**.

To **Resize** a picture:
Highlight it and use the mouse to drag a corner handle.

I Create your own repeat pattern using a stamp or a picture from the Clip Art gallery.

Most Clip Art collections have interesting pictures or shapes. Make a repeat pattern with a shape and use it to decorate a poem or a story you have written. Group the shapes to make them easier to use.

II Put a tick next to the sentences that are correct and a cross next to those that are incorrect.

a A pattern is a design that is repeated. ☐

b Clip Art shapes can be used to create patterns using **Format** and **Font**. ☐

c If you highlight a shape, you can move it or resize it using the handles. ☐

d It is easier to use a pattern to decorate your writing if the shapes are joined together as a group. ☐

e To join the shapes, you need to use the tools on the **Standard** toolbar. ☐

Symmetrical patterns

Painting and **Drawing** programs have special tools to make it easier to produce symmetrical patterns.

- Open **Paint.**
- Use the **Shape** and **Line** tools to draw a simple design.
- Fill the shape with colour and **Save As** 'tile1' (remember to **Save As** a jpeg file).
- Use the **Select** tool and drag a dotted box around the design.
- Open the **Edit** menu and choose **Copy.**
- Open the **Edit** menu and choose **Paste.**
- Drag the pasted image to the side of the original (enlarge the canvas by dragging the corner arrow if you need to).
- While the design is still highlighted with the dotted line, open the **Image** menu and left mouse click on **Flip.** Click on **Flip horizontal** and **OK** to make a symmetrical pattern.

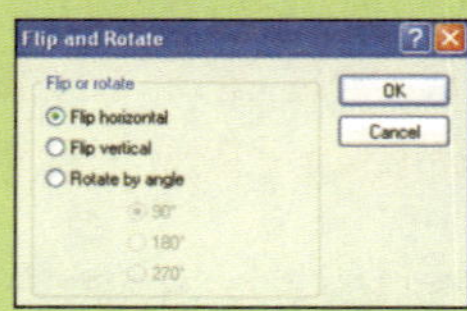

- **Save** your design **As** 'tile2'.

I Create your own symmetrical pattern.

- Use the **Paint** tools to create a design for an Islamic tile and **Save As** 'istile1'.
- **Select**, **Copy**, **Paste** and **Flip** the design horizontally and **Save As** a jpeg 'istile2'.
- Now **Select**, **Copy**, **Paste** and **Flip** both tiles vertically – remember to enlarge the canvas by dragging the corner arrow so that you have room to paste.
- **Save As** 'istile3'. **Save As** a jpeg file.
- **Print** the design.

II Draw a line to match the action with the menu in which you can find it.

a Flip	b Copy and Paste	c Save As
File menu	Image menu	Edit menu

d Why is it a good idea to save each stage of the pattern with a different name?

____

____

The whole picture

When designing a poster or a newspaper, it helps to look at the whole page. The **Zoom** tool lets you 'zoom in' to get a close-up view (100%) or 'zoom out' to see the whole page.

Use **Zoom** to check to see if headings stand out and if pictures are in the right place. While viewing the whole page, you can move text and pictures until you are happy with the layout.

To view the whole page:

- Open **View** and choose **Zoom** or left mouse click on this button .
- Select **Whole Page.**

To go back to the normal view:

- Use **View** and **Zoom** and select 100%.

The **Zoom** shortcut on the toolbar lets you select different views, including **Whole Page** by clicking on the down arrow and scrolling down the options.

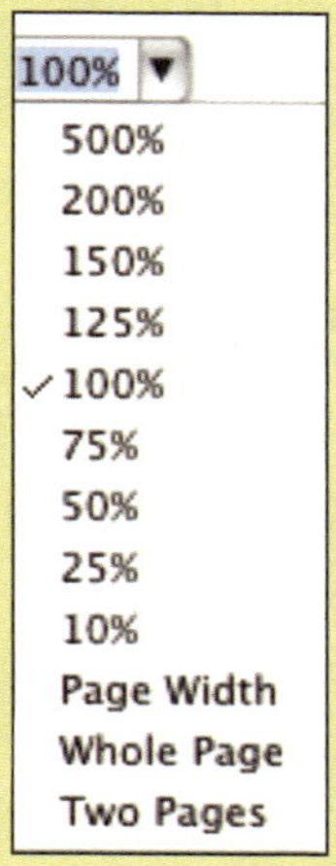

Quick reminder

To move a graphic:

- Highlight it.
- Use the mouse to drag the graphic to a new place on the page.

I Use this slogan to design a poster for recycled newspaper:

Read and Recycle

- Add two or three Clip Art pictures.
- Make the text stand out using different fonts, sizes or styles.
- Use **Zoom** to see the whole page. Resize and move the pictures to organise the layout of the poster.

II Write down how the text appears on the screen when you:

a Open **View**, and **Zoom** 200%. ______________________

b Open **View** and **Zoom** to whole page. ______________________

Can you see the whole page when you:

c Open **View**, and **Zoom** 75%? ______________________

d Use the shortcut button and **Zoom** 50%? ______________________

e When would you use **Zoom**? Underline your choices.

to organise a newspaper page *to reorder a story* *to design a poster*

Collecting data

The best way to gather information for a **database** is with a questionnaire. Here is an example:

Travel to school

1. Are you a boy or girl? ____________
2. How old are you? ________________
3. How do you get to school? bus car walk
4. How long does your journey take?

   5–10 min 10–20 min 20–30 min more than 30 min
5. Do you travel with an adult? Y/N ____________

A questionnaire has questions with:

- Word or number answers.
- Yes or No answers.
- Multiple choice answers (sometimes a multiple choice lets you give more than one answer).

This questionnaire was designed for a whole school, but you can design one for a small group of people as well. Here are some ideas: favourite foods, hobbies, favourite TV programmes, games people play.

I **Plan and type a questionnaire with five questions about the journeys people make in the morning to school or to work.**

Include questions that need:

- Word or number answers.
- Yes or No answers.
- Multiple choice answers.

Try the questionnaire on a member of your family to see how well it works. Change or add questions after you have tested your questionnaire, if you need to.

II **What type of answers do these questions need? Choose from: *word*, *number*, *yes/no*, *multiple choice*.**

a Which of these sandwiches do you like – cheese, ham, tuna, egg? ____________

b Do you like butter on your sandwich? ____________

c Do you prefer white or brown bread? ____________

d How old are you? ____________

e What is your favourite sandwich? ____________

f Do you have sandwiches at dinnertime in school? ____________

Designing a database

Data collected from a questionnaire can be used to create **Fields** and **Records** for a database file.

To create a database for your 'Journeys' questionnaire:

JOURNEYS : Table

Field Name	Data Type
boy or girl	Text
age	Number
bus, car, walk, bike	Text
how long does it take in minutes?	Number
do you travel with an adult?	Yes/No

- Open **Access** and choose **Blank Database.**
- Give your database the file name: 'JOURNEYS' and choose **Create.**
- Choose **Open** from the next box.
- Type 'boy or girl' in the **Field Name** column.
- Open the options box in the **Data Type** column, using the **down arrow** and choose **Text.**
- Continue to add the **Field Names** and **Data Types** shown in the table.
- **Save as** 'JOURNEYS' and **Close** the box ☒.
- Choose **No** to the next box.
- Double click the left mouse button on the table called JOURNEYS to open it. Add the information from your questionnaire.

I Create a 'Favourite Food' database using Access.

a Create a questionnaire and collect answers from ten people.

Boy/male or girl/female	Age	Vegetarian	Favourite meal	Favourite drink

b Create a simple database in **Access**, using your questions for the **Field Names**.

c Choose a **Data Type** for each field name to show what type of answers you have been given. **Save** your work. **Open** the table and add the data you have collected to the table.

II Answer the following questions about organising data.

a Choose a **Data Type** to match each field:

Field	**Data type**
Name	________________
Age	________________
I travel on my own	________________

b Explain how you would sort the journeys so that the shortest journeys are at the top of the list.

____

____

Graphs and charts

A graph is a quick and easy way to view information.

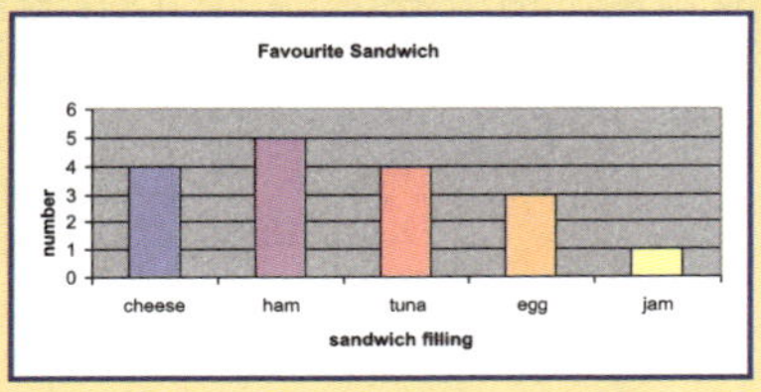

Column graphs and bar charts show or compare numbers.

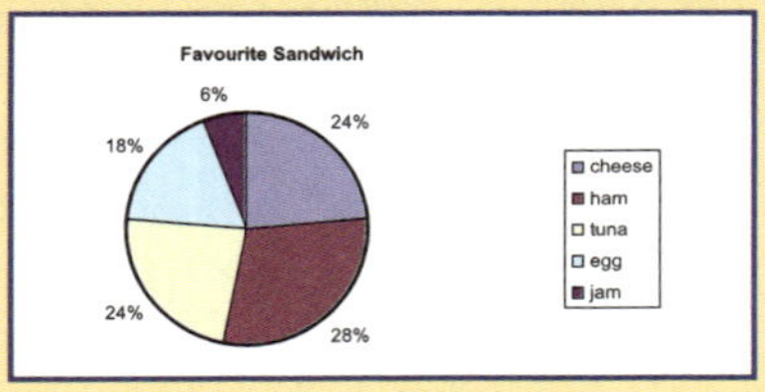

Pie charts show percentages.

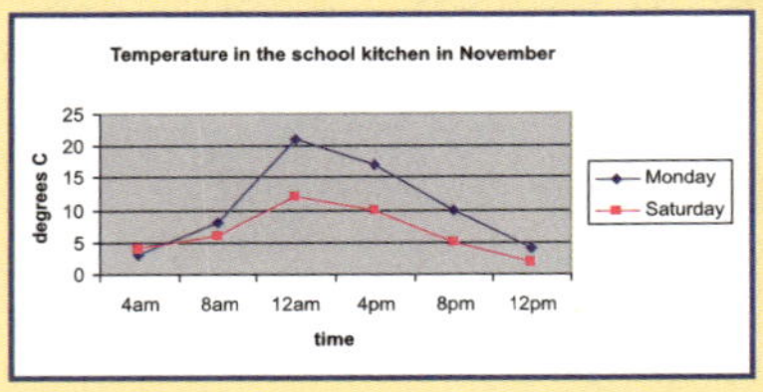

Line graphs record changes that have happened over time.

Practise drawing a column graph using **Excel**:

- Open **Excel**, type in this data about favourite sandwiches and highlight it.

B	C	D	E	F
cheese	ham	tuna	egg	jam
4	5	4	3	1

- Open the **Chart Wizard** .
- Choose **Column Graph**, then **Next** and **Next** again until you see a screen with these menus:

◇	A	B	C	D	E	F
1	Titles	Axes	Gridlines	Legend	Data Labels	Data Table

Give the chart a title.

Add data labels by ticking the boxes.

To see the graph, **'Place chart as an object on sheet 1'** when you get to the last box and left mouse click on **Finish**.

I **Open Excel and type in this data.**

◇	A	B	C	D
1	gymnastics	games	dancing	apparatus
2	3	7	5	10

a Highlight the data and create a **Column Graph** using **Chart Wizard** .

b Add a title of your choice: *'Favourite PE lessons'* or *'Favourite Hobbies'*

c Choose and add a label for the X axis: *dances* or *PE lessons*

d Choose and add a label for the Y axis: *number of children* or *number of PE lessons*

II **Look in Chart Wizard. Name these types of graphs or charts.**

a  ______________________

b  ______________________

c  ______________________

d  ______________________

Pie charts

Pie charts are round. They are used to compare information. Here are three charts for classes 1, 2 and 3.

◇	A	B
1		Class 1
2	Girls	16
3	Boys	8

◇	A	B
1		Class 2
2	Girls	14
3	Boys	7

◇	A	B
1		Class 3
2	Girls	12
3	Boys	16

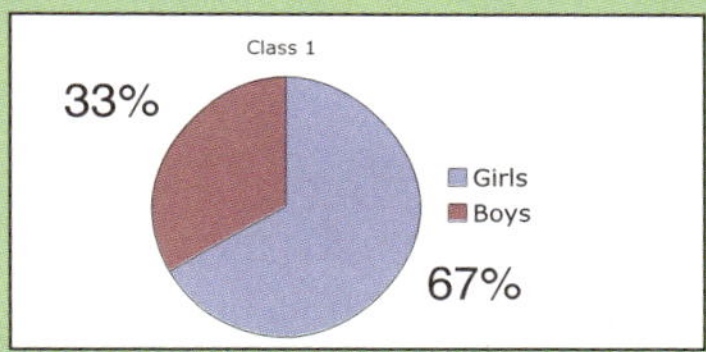

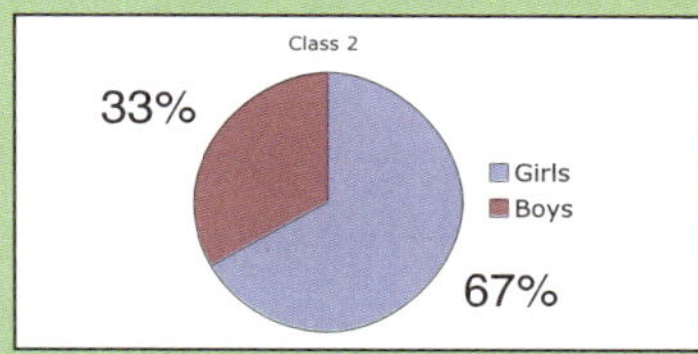

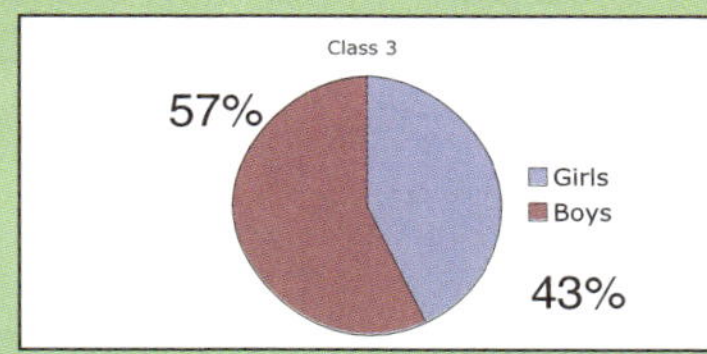

Even though the numbers are different in each class, the pie charts are the same for Classes 1 and 2 – for every boy there are two girls.

To make a pie chart:

◇	A	B
1		Class 1
2	Girls	16
3	Boys	8

- Open **Excel**, type in this data and highlight it.
- Open **Chart Wizard** and select a **Pie Chart**.
- Choose **Next** until you come to the menu box with labels.
- Add a **Title** and **Data Labels** (tick **percentages** and **category name**).
- To change the font, size and colour of the text on the finished chart, highlight the text box and use Times ▼ 12 ▼ and A ▾.

I Open Excel and type in this data showing how Sam spent his day.

a Use the **Chart Wizard** to create a pie chart.

b Add **Data Labels** and change the text size and font.

◇	A	B
1	school	6
2	eating	2
3	playing games	2
4	watching TV	3
5	sleeping	10
6	homework	1

II Tick the charts which are pie charts out of the following.

a

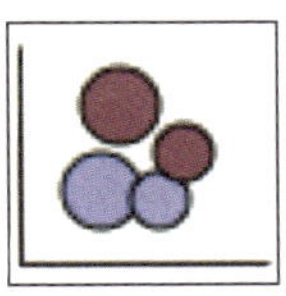

☐

b

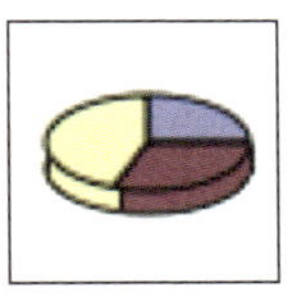

☐

c

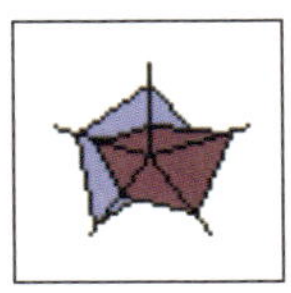

☐

d

☐

e When would you use a pie chart?

☐ *To look at how you spend your pocket money.*

☐ *To show the height and weight of five people.*

Line graphs

Line graphs are often used to plot the results of a science experiment when measurements are taken over a period of time.

A shadow was measured at different times during the day.

◇	A	B	C	D	E	F	G
1	9am	10am	11am	12am	1pm	2pm	3pm
2	62	54	32	10	37	58	65
3							

This line graph shows the results of the experiment.

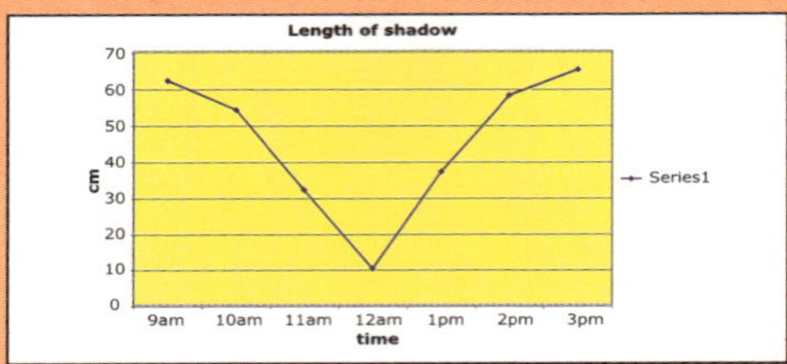

By using a line graph, it is possible to guess the length of the shadow for those times when measurements were not taken.

To create a line graph:

- Open **Excel**, type in the data and highlight it.
- Open the **Chart Wizard** and select **Line Graph**.
- Follow the instructions on-screen, and add labels for the Title and Data.
- To change the background or line colour of the graph, left click on it and choose a colour using: .

I **Open Excel and type in this data to show the height of a plant in cm as it grew from a seed.**

◇	A	B	C	D	E	F
1	2.5.03	16.5.03	2.6.03	16.6.03	30.6.03	6.7.03
2	0	1	4	8	11	16
3						

Use the **Chart Wizard** to create a line graph.

II **Dan cycled with his dad to a friend's house. Here is a graph to show their journey.**

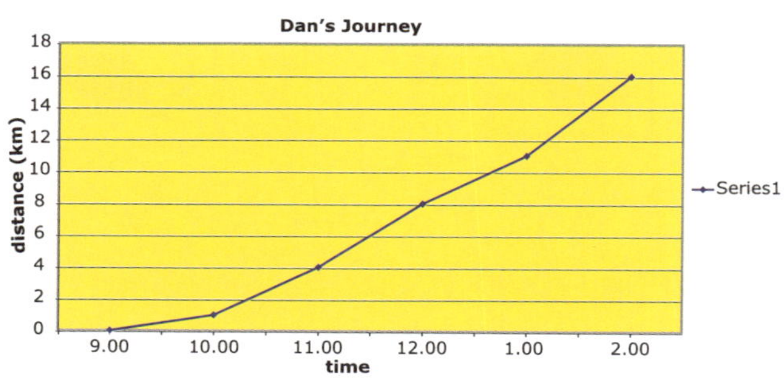

a Why do you think Dan used a line graph?

____

b How far would they have travelled at 10.30?

____

Branching databases

Branching databases are used to sort and organise information.

Here are some elves to show us how **branching databases** work. Let's imagine we can ask them some questions to find out who they are.

Are you wearing an orange hat?

Yes Jim, Nim, Kim	No Lim, Mim, Tim

Do you have blue trousers?

Yes Nim	No Jim, Kim

Do you have green shoes?

Yes Jim	No Kim

Do you have a blue hat?

Yes Lim	No Mim, Tim

Do you have orange trousers?

Yes Mim	No Tim

By asking a question with a yes/no answer, the elves are sorted into two sets. When there are two or more names in a box, a different question with a yes/no answer separates them. Using the tree diagram, we can now identify each elf by the clothes they are wearing. See if you can identify each elf.

I **Create a paper-based branching database to sort and organise the musical instruments in the box.**

flute	drum	guitar	piano	trumpet	violin

Use questions that give a yes/no answer, e.g. 'Is it a brass instrument?'

II **Here is some information about three more elves. Using the tree diagram above, whose box would you put them in?**

a Berty – orange hat, orange trousers, yellow shoes ____________

b Sammy – green hat, green trousers, yellow shoes ____________

c Lonny – orange hat, yellow trousers, green shoes ____________

d Think of a question with a yes/no answer to separate Lonny and the elf in his box.

____

The world wide web

The **world wide web** has millions of information pages. To help you to find information, there are special websites called **Search Engines** with **Search Boxes.**

To Search for information:

- Connect to the **Internet.** In the **Address Box** type: www.yahooligans.yahoo.com
- Type the word 'rugby' in the **Search Box.** Click **Search** with the left mouse button.

rugby	Search

Words typed in a search box are called key words. Search engines find links to other websites using key words. Use these links to visit a page and find information.

rugby + six nations	Search

To make your search more accurate use +.

I Connect to the Internet, and go to a search engine website and try these searches.

a In the search box, type: Queen.
Circle the number of websites listed. *fewer than 50* *50–100* *more than 100*

If more than 100 write the number here ________

b In the search box, type: Queen + Elizabeth
Circle the number of websites listed. *fewer than 20* *20–50* *more than 50*

If more than 50 write the number here ________

c In the search box, type: Queen + Elizabeth + II
Circle the number of websites listed. *fewer than 10* *10–20* *more than 20*

If more than 20 write the number here ________

II Which website would you visit if you typed these key words? Tick the website you would choose.

a Search for: Sheffield + England

- ☐ **Sheffield, England, UK – tourist guide**
  A guide and information for the city and the surrounding area
- ☐ **Sheffield**
  The Sheffield School of Business

b Search for: Birmingham + England

- ☐ **Birmingham Zoo**
  Alabama, USA
- ☐ **Birmingham City Council**
  Official city site of Birmingham, UK

c Search for: The Queen + England

- ☐ **The Official Queen website**
  Latest news about the Queen rock musical
- ☐ **Official site of the British Monarchy**
  This includes details of the Queen's speeches and her visits around the world

E-mail extras

An **e-mail** is an electronic letter. When you send an e-mail you can add an **attachment**. An attachment can be a photo, a piece of writing or a sound clip that has been saved as a file.

- Open your e-mail software and your mailbox and click **New**.
- Write your message in the message box.

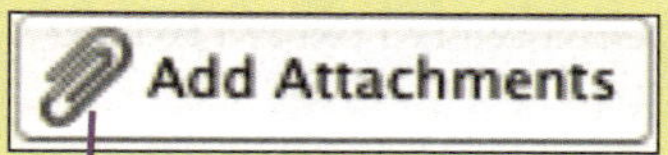

To add an attachment, left mouse click on the paperclip.

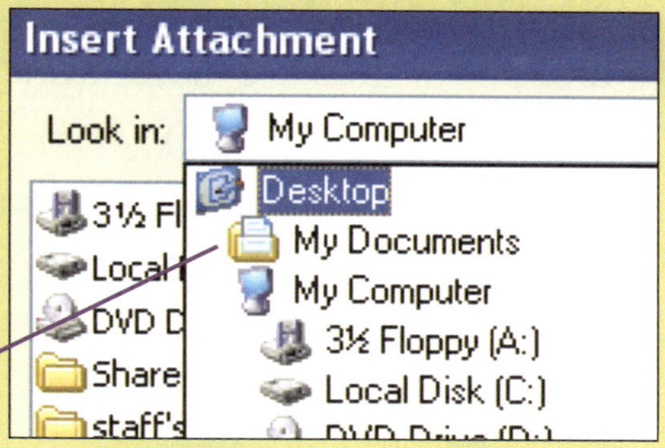

Look in your folder, highlight the file you want to attach and left mouse click on **Attach**.

To open an attachment in your mailbox, open the e-mail and double click on the attachment with the left mouse button. E-mails are sometimes used to spread computer viruses, so only open e-mails from people you know. Viruses can damage the files saved on your computer.

I Send a special poem to your friends.

a Write a poem and **Save** it in your folder.

b Open your e-mail software and mailbox.

c Write an e-mail to your friends and attach the poem.

d Connect to the **Internet** and send it.

II Complete the sentences by circling the correct ending.

a An attachment is *a file* *a paperclip.*

b To add an attachment you need to browse *your documents* *the Internet.*

c You can *only send* *only receive* *send and receive attachments.*

d What would you do if you received an e-mail from someone you did not know? *open it* *delete it* *ask an adult.*

Explain your answer:

____

____

Screen turtles

Screen turtles work in the same way as floor turtles:

- They obey the same commands: **right (rt)**; **left (lt)**; **forward (fd)**; **back (bk)**; **lt 90°** ($\frac{1}{4}$ turn anti-clockwise); **rt 90°** ($\frac{1}{4}$ turn clockwise).
- They move in different directions without drawing if you type the command: **pen up**.
- They draw lines when they move if you type the command: **pen down**.

The steps they take are 'screen unit steps' which are much smaller than floor turtle steps. 50 screen turtle 'steps' would draw a line about this long:

Here are the instructions to draw an equilateral triangle. Press the **enter** key after each instruction:

```
pen down
fd 200
rt 120
fd 200
rt 120
fd 200
rt 120
```

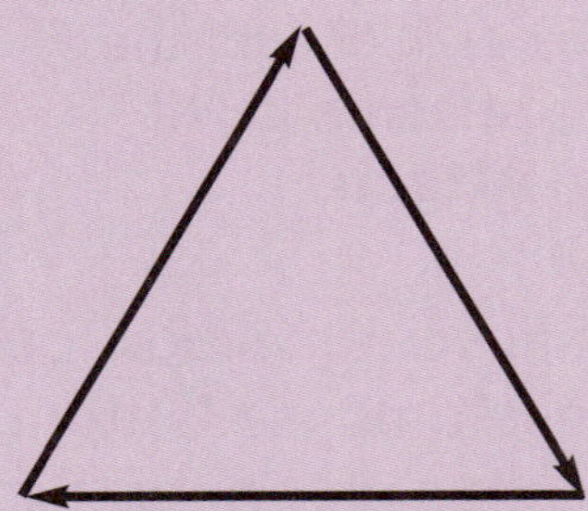

I Type a set of instructions in a new Word document, for a screen turtle to draw:

a A triangle with equal sides of 150, each turn = 120.

b A hexagon with equal sides of 150, each turn = 60.

c A rectangle with 2 sides of 150 and 2 sides of 100, each turn = 90.

II What are these regular shapes?

a

```
fd 150      fd 150
rt 90       rt 90
fd 75       fd 75
rt 90       rt 90
```

____

b

```
fd 150      fd 150
rt 72       rt 72
fd 150      fd 150
rt 72       rt 72
fd 150
rt 72
```

____

c

```
fd 100      fd 100
rt 45       rt 45
fd 100      fd 100
rt 45       rt 45
fd 100      fd 100
rt 45       rt 45
fd 100      fd 100
rt 45       rt 45
```

____

Regular shapes

Instead of typing a new instruction for every line that you want the turtle to draw, it is quicker to give the turtle all the instructions at once. You are also less likely to make a mistake!

When the turtle is drawing a regular shape, the instructions are often repeated. The turtle understands the word **Repeat** so to instruct the turtle to draw a square, type:

```
Repeat 4 [fd 100 rt 90]
```

Here are some more examples:

To draw a triangle:	To draw a hexagon:	To draw an octagon
Repeat 3 [fd 120 rt 120]	Repeat 6 [fd 100 rt 60]	Repeat 8 [fd 100 rt 45]

When you add up the numbers (degrees) for each turn, the total for regular shapes comes to 360. To find how many degrees to turn the turtle, divide 360 by the number of sides in the shape.

I Use Repeat to type instructions for these shapes:

a A triangle with equal sides of 200.

b A hexagon with equal sides of 150.

c A decagon (10 sides) with equal sides of 70.

d A pentagon with equal sides of 115.

II Answer these questions about shapes, as drawn by screen turtles.

a If a shape had 36 regular sides, how many degrees would you turn the turtle to draw each new side?

____

b If a shape had 20 regular sides, how many degrees would you turn the turtle to draw each new side?

____

c How could you make this shape: Repeat 3 [fd 120 rt 120], bigger?

____

____

Turtle flowers

The screen turtle understands the word **Repeat**. You can also teach it to understand the word **square**:

```
to square
repeat 4 [fd 100 rt 90]
end
```

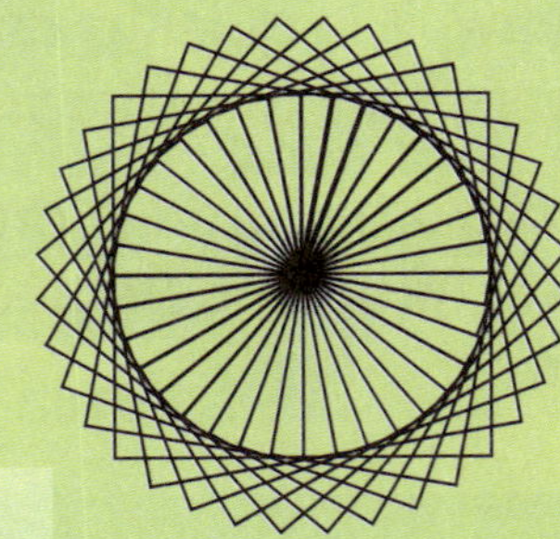

You can teach the turtle other names too:

```
to triangle
repeat 3 [fd 100 rt 120]
end
```

```
to circle
repeat 360 [fd 1 rt 1]
end
```

Now the turtle has learnt these words, you can give the turtle instructions to use them and produce a flower pattern:

```
repeat 36 [square rt 10]
```

The instructions tell the turtle to draw a square 36 times, but for each new square, the turtle must turn 10° clockwise.

I Complete the procedures to teach the turtle how to draw these shapes.

a

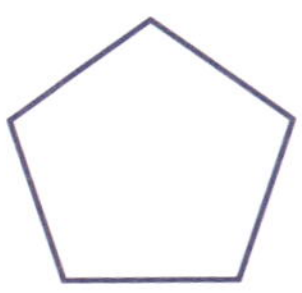

Name of shape:

____

repeat ______

[fd 100 rt ______]

end

b

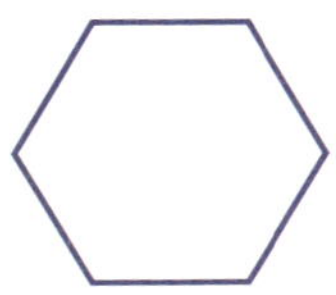

Name of shape:

____

repeat ______

[fd 100 rt ______]

end

c

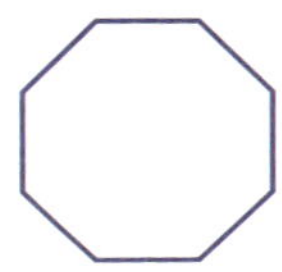

Name of shape:

____

repeat ______

[fd 100 rt ______]

end

II Write the procedures for a triangle and a circle, then use these to write instructions to draw a crystal flower.

a TRIANGLE

____

____

____

____

b CIRCLE

____

____

____

____

Keyboard practice and shortcuts

A keyboard has letter, number and punctuation keys. It also has some special keys:

- **shift key** ⇧

  Hold the **shift key** and tap a **letter key** to make a capital letter.

- **control key** Ctrl

  Use the **control key** for some keyboard shortcuts.

Useful shortcuts:

Press and hold **Ctrl** with these keys:

Ctrl + P to **Print**
Ctrl + S to **Save**
Ctrl + X to **Cut** highlighted text and images
Ctrl + C to **Copy** highlighted text and images
Ctrl + V to **Paste** what is on the clipboard

I Use the shift key to type every other letter of the alphabet as a capital letter.

a B c D e F g H i J k L m N o P q R s T u V w X y Z

a Start with a lower case a, then a capital B and finish with a capital Z.

b Do it again starting with a capital A and a lower case b.

c Draw a circle shape with the **Drawing** tools and use **Ctrl C** and **Ctrl V** to copy it four times. Drag the five circles into a row and **Group** them using the **Select**, **Draw/Group** Tools (look at page 14 to remember how to do this). Use **Ctrl C** and **Ctrl V** to make four rows and **Group** them again. Use **Ctrl S** to **Save** the blank grid and **Ctrl P** to print it. Take turns with a friend to play three-in-a-row.

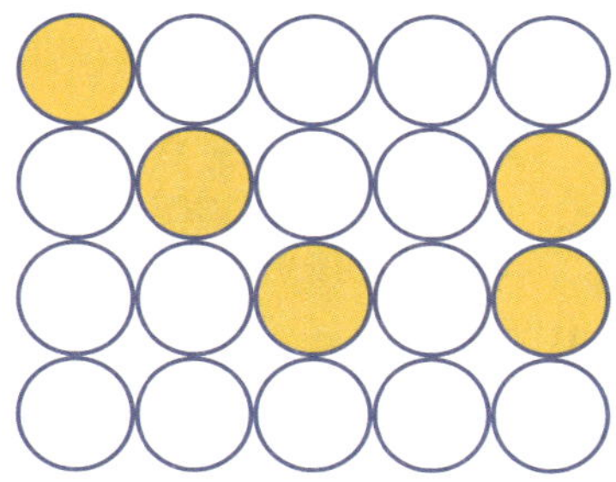

II Identify the shortcut.

a To **Cut** highlighted text and images:	*Ctrl + C*	*Ctrl + X*	*Ctrl + S*
b To **Copy** highlighted text and images:	*Ctrl + C*	*Ctrl + X*	*Ctrl + S*
c To **Paste** what's on the clipboard:	*Ctrl + C*	*Ctrl + X*	*Ctrl + V*
d To **Print**:	*Ctrl + C*	*Ctrl + X*	*Ctrl + P*

Look in the menus on the menu bar and find the shortcut for:

e Undo typing: ____________________

f Which menu did you use? ____________________

ANSWERS

Page 2

II **a** Formatting
b Standard
c Standard
d Formatting
e Drawing
f Formatting

Page 3

II **a** 'Files' should be circled.
b So that you don't lose it if something happens to the program or your computer.
c You can find it again easily.

Page 4

II **a** Open the Format menu then open the Font menu.
b The font, size, colour, underlining and effects.
c Party Invitation, Saturday 27th September and Dining Dinosaurs Fun Den.

Page 5

I b, e, c, a, d

II **a** 
b 
c X
d V

Page 6

I The answers may vary, but as a guide the following words should be circled:
a chilly, frosty
b lovely, fine
c enjoyable, excellent
d cheerful, contented
e gloomy, miserable

II Here are some examples – but you may have different words that mean the same: wonderful, exciting, happy, sad.

Page 7

I Danny's class were having a competition to desine a moneybox, so Danny asked if he could look in his Dad's shed for some idaes. His freind Peter came around to help. At the bottom of an old cuboard, Danny found just what he was looking four.

The spell checker missed: four

II **a** This means there is a spelling mistake.
b This means the words you used might not make sense.

Page 8

I Words changed:
a I, my
b she, her

II To **Find** and **Replace** a word, open the **Edit** menu and choose **Replace**. Type the word you want to change in the **'Find** what' box. Type the new word in the '**Replace** with' box. Click **Replace**. **Find** and **Replace** finds and changes words easily, without **missing** any!

Page 9

II **a** left **b** centre **c** right

Page 10

II **a** Format should be circled.
b You can make it bold, italic, underlined, change its style, give it different effects and change how far in it is indented.

Page 11

II **Across:** **1** highlight **4** dashes **5** labels **7** dots
Down: **2** insert **3** handle **4** drawing **6** box

Page 12

II The following should be circled:
a columns
b three
c make the text look more important
d headlines

Page 13

II **a** Insert a picture from the Clip Art gallery or Clip Art CD-ROM; scan in a picture using a scanner; download a picture from a digital camera.
b You need special software.
c Open Clip Art from the Insert menu using Picture, from Clip Art. Type a word in the Search For box and press the enter key.

Page 14

II **a** Select (highlight) a shape or object on-screen.
b Fill with colour.
c Add a text box.
d Group several shapes to merge them into one image.
e Choose a line colour.
f Choose a font colour.

Page 15

II **1** scanner
2 start
3 send (across), scan (down)
4 jpeg
5 repair